To:

With Love:

365 Ways . . . 365 Days

Love Blurbs
Loving Simply & Simply Loving

Paris Angel

Copyright © 2012 by Paris Angel.

ISBN: 978-0-6158-7801-0

All rights reserved. No part of this book may be reproduced or transmitted in any form or by any means, electronic or mechanical, including photocopying, recording, or by any information storage and retrieval system, without permission in writing from the copyright owner.

This is a work of fiction. Names, characters, places and incidents either are the product of the author's imagination or are used fictitiously, and any resemblance to any actual persons, living or dead, events, or locales is entirely coincidental.

This book was printed in the United States of America.

To order additional copies of this book, contact:
www.answersfromparis.com

DEDICATION

This book is dedicated to all the couples who simply love each other and love each other simply; it is not intended for anyone to nitpick about all of the things that their partner does not do but rather to glorify with deep meaning, and complexity loves true simplicity!

Keep it real and stay in love; it's simpler than one thinks.

Loving Simply & Simply Loving

Paris Angel

SPECIAL THANKS

With all the love a heart can hold, I thank my family and friends. For those of you who have supported me in this adventure of finally getting this in writing, you know who you are.

Special thanks to my husband, Iad, for being the greatest inspiration and shining example of someone who really learned to express their love and continues to do so every day. Thank you for believing in me and helping me believe in myself.

To Stephanie my daughter for helping keep life in order around me so that my brain could think clearly and have space for creativity.

To Meonah my daughter also for helping keep life in order around me, for taking care of me when I needed it, and for all the tea and energy drinks that helped get me through this endeavor.

Thank you to the couples who love each other enough to provide me inspiration and include their blurbs in my book; I am moved deeply to see people love simply and simply love.

PROLOGUE

I'm not going to make this too lengthy, so bear with me, allowing me this moment to share some love with you.

It started with a few simple words a long time ago when I was a kid. I was an only child at this time in my life. I talked a lot and was very opinionated for my age and smart for my age too. I would like to thank my father for that as he encouraged me to be a freethinker as long as I wasn't deliberately contradicting him . . . (LOL). It seemed as though when I was young, I was always offering up a kind solution or possible compromise to situations grown-ups seemed to be getting themselves into.

I had a great interest in what made people tick and why they did the things they did. When you're a child and you do this, you get told to shut up by a lot of adults, and then there was my father in the background laughing at his friends who were trying to figure out how to deal with me. Again, Dad, thank you so much. You made me the strong-willed, capable, creative person I am today.

Moving forward, in preadolescence, I moved in with my mother where there was a drastic change. Unlike living with my father who had a very good job and I never wanted for anything, in fact I lived in excess, not to mention I was the only child, moving in with my mother not only did I often wonder where the next meal would come from, but now suddenly, I was the oldest of four. I guess you could say I learned to share and love the hard way . . . trial by fire.

Paris Angel

The most interesting thing about not having money is the luxuries that money provides are not there so we did not have a lot of modern forms of entertainment that other children had; being the oldest, oftentimes, it became my responsibility to come up with something for everyone to do. This was when I began to tell stories; I was basically the household television. This was also when I learned about creative interaction with those you love, I learned about compromise, and I learned a little love goes a long way.

This however did not save me from two failed marriages, for I found that loving a significant other is not enough to make it work. Now over twenty-eight years in the bar, restaurant, and entertainment industry, I have been exposed to and interacted with, I would say, hundreds of relationships; and I have learned so much . . . like I said, I like to share. When I was a kid, it was called talking too much, and I was told to shut up; but as an adult, people seemed to like to share with me their problems, and I really enjoyed sharing my thoughts with them.

Paris Angel

The interesting part is some people applied some of the conversations we had to their life, and it greatly improved their relationship with their significant other. They were very grateful to me. How many times I have heard the words "you should write a book" I cannot begin to tell you.

So in looking back, I realize the one thing many conversations had in common involving relationships between people is how complicated they become, how the simplicity of loving one another, the feeling that the other person loves you back, seems to be stripped away by the harsh reality and responsibilities of life.

Really, I oftentimes thought in the back of my mind that many of these people did not recognize all the signs of the other person loving them. You see, I believe that people love in their own and independent manner but, at the same time, need to understand what their partner feels are signs of love, then somehow between these two realities, they learn to express love to one another yet still being able to express their love in their independent way, adding color variations from the palette of their loved one so the loved one recognizes the doings as love.

Paris Angel

It is so much simpler than we make it; there is so much less stress when you allow love to be fertilized by the simple things.

Looking back in time, just letting you wear their favorite leather jacket was a sign they loved you, and you wearing it was a sign you loved them; it was a courting ritual, but it meant love. Now look at how simple that was, times have become so complicated; we shouldn't let the times dictate our hearts.

365 WAYS... 365 DAYS

1   You say pretty much everything is made better if I am involved; it feels good to know I enhance your world.

2   You kiss me before either of us leave to go anyplace, even for small errands like the grocery store.

3   You accept life's changes as they come, accepting me as I change with life, reassuring me that change is not bad. It's not about being how we were when we met that will keep us together and in love; but rather about deciding what we will be and become together that makes our future.

4   You never go to sleep mad at me.

5   You prefer to sit beside me wherever we are, whether it is at home or in public.

6   Although you may not understand what I am feeling when I'm having a hard time, you are sympathetic to my feelings. You look past yourself, feel for me, and help me through it.

7   You always call after work to see if I need anything on your way home.

8   You share the remote.

9   You understand my obsession with cars, so to spend time with me, you will join me in the grease, tools, and car parts with a dinner delivery or under the hood for a beer and a little kissin'.

10   If you are able, you will call me every day on your break just to say hi; you say hearing my voice in the middle of the day makes the rest of your day so much easier.

11 When it is my *TOM*, you are not shy about picking up supplies for me.

12 You bring me flowers at work.

Wolf Woman

13 You will always eat whatever I want to eat, you don't care about what you are eating, you care about if I am enjoying what I am eating because you enjoy all food and I do not.

14   You know what I'm saying with my toothbrush in my mouth.

15   You kiss me good night every night.

16   You are always there for me, and that's what friends are about.

17   You tolerate my pet even though you can't stand it.

18   When I come home from work late at night, if I've had a bad night, you will wake up and talk it out with me.

19   You remind me of my strengths regularly, and it makes me feel better about myself.

20   You always say "I love you" first before we hang up the phone; if you forget to say it, you will call right back to tell me.

21   You kiss me every day before leaving for work.

22   There is something very strong inside of me that pulls me to be beside you, moves me to be part of your life, draws me to where you are, to be near you, and to listen to what you think and how you feel.

23   You invite me to sit in your lap often.

24 You steal my pillows during the night.

25 You laugh when I do something stupid, rather than getting mad at me, somehow you find it entertaining.

26 Whenever you see me struggling with something in life, you ask me if I need to talk about it or lightly nudge for information to get me talking because you know it makes me feel better to talk about it.

27 You will always be the one to get up after we've gotten comfortable in bed to get whatever has been forgotten, like the lights, aspirin, water, windows, and doors just whatever; you are the one to take care of it.

28 If I come to bed naked, you can't leave me alone no matter how tired you are.

29 You tell me often that you love my smile, my eyes, and the smell of my hair.

30   You still remember what I was wearing the first day we met.

31   The end of my workday is much later than yours, so I come to bed after you are already sleeping; when I climb into bed, you moan a little, make a deep sigh of comfort, and I see you smile in your sleep.

32   No matter who hurts my feelings or what makes me cry, you take my side in the moment and work out the details later.

33 Whenever I have a rough day, you say, "I'm sorry you had a bad day." I know you mean this, and it makes me feel better.

34 All these years of being together, and you still grunt when you see me in tight jeans.

35 If I tell you I love you when you are sound asleep, from the depths of your sleep, you will say, "I love you too, baby!"

36   You do not use my good scissors for things they are not designed for, i.e., paper scissors are for paper, etc. I know that this means you respect me.

37   You get a soft and happy look in your eyes as you approach to hug or kiss me.

38   No matter what the conditions of the day at your work are, you will take my call even if all you can say is "Baby, I can't talk right now. Can I call you back?"

39   You told me the best part of every day is when you get to come home to me.

40   You would rather spend time with me watching movies, playing games, or taking a drive on your days off versus worrying about what's for dinner, how clean the house is, or whether or not our yard looks like the neighbor's yard.

41   You can't make friends with people who don't like me; you told me those people were a waste of your time and a bad emotional investment.

42   When I lose something important, you always find it. If you don't have time to look for it, you will say, "Don't worry, I'll find it when I get home." Funny part is, you almost always find whatever I've lost.

43   While I cook in the kitchen, you come keep me company; you will make us something to drink, start conversation, play music that I enjoy listening to, offer to prep food, or run to the store if I need anything for the meal. Once you are served your dinner, you wait for me so we can eat together.

44   You often walk up behind me and kiss me on my shoulders.

45   You appreciate it when I get a pedicure or a manicure; you always notice and compliment.

46   When you find me uncovered in the night, you cover me back up.

47 It seems like no matter how many nice pens I have, you will always bring me another nice pen as a little gift.

48 When I do something silly, maybe even stupid in the eyes of other people, you never look down on me and you don't find it stupid; in fact, you find me amusing and will say, "I love you soooooo much," then you smile at me.

49   You always want to shower with me; if you think there is even a remote chance we are going to shower together, you will wait on your shower.

50   You make a regular habit out of doing things that make me smile.

51 With over 100 colors of lip gloss, you will stand by with a smile on your face while I buy yet another color of lip gloss I think I don't have. Before I apply the new gloss, you will ask for a kiss; I always give that kiss. It dawned on me that maybe because I always grant the kiss before the gloss application was the reason you always smile when I buy lip gloss. To you, lip gloss equals kisses; this could also be why you point out lip gloss when we are shopping.

52   You chuckle when you see my cleavage. This could be lust, but after 11+ years, you're still doing it; whether it is love of cleavage or love of me, it is still love.

53   You doodle my name and draw little hearts on random pieces of paper while you talk on the phone.

54   Whether away on a trip, away at work, or just away on an errand, I always feel this little sense of something missing; life's balance is not perfect when you are away. You don't have to be in my lap, but just your presence within the same general proximity of my existence seems to create a peaceful harmony.

55   You once told me that every piece of your

life is yet another part of *our* life.

56   You get up in the morning and pack my lunch, make my breakfast, and see me out the door.

Marie

57 You, being a submariner, will be gone months at a time [underway]. The very little contact you get is e-mail. Prior to every underway, I will write you notes; one note for every day you will be gone [estimated]. At each shift's end, before you go to sleep, you read a note. It is a little piece of me that you can have every day, and you told me it is the best part of any day.

58 After making us a drink, you always wait for that first sip until I have chosen what we should toast to.

59   You challenge me in areas I need to grow with love and understanding.

Wolf Woman

60   If we shower together, you will stand in the back of the shower to give me space; this is what you tell me. Truth be known, you do this to watch me shower, I'm sure.

61   You iron my uniforms.

62   I work a full-time job and would have very little time to spend with the family if I cleaned on my days off; you see to it the house is kept clean so that we can have quality family time.

63   You respect my personal grooming apparatuses and supplies; you always ask before you use them.

64   You bathe the dog on bath day.

65 You write me little love notes and put them in my lunch box, briefcase, or shirt pocket so I will find them during my day at work.

66 You put up with me and try to comfort me when I am cranky; you don't antagonize the situation or think it's funny.

67 You appreciate my sense of humor.

68 You always notice when I trim my hair.

69   You remember my birthday every year and always do something to make it special.

70   You think the things other people find dysfunctional about me interesting, exciting, and a valuable part of who I am.

71   You think I'm sexy in my pajamas... and by no means are my pajamas sexy.

72   It doesn't matter to you where we spend the holiday as long as I have no stress and we are together.

73   You tell me, "I don't care where I live. What makes any place a home to me is when I come home, you are on the other side of the door."

74   You happily watch the kids to send me on a friend's night out because you know I need to cut loose.

75   You are very complimentary to my mother's cooking and eat every bite of it as if you love it. (My mother is a terrible cook.)

76　　You are always willing to drop whatever you are doing whenever you are doing it (as long it is something you can walk away from) to become sexually involved with me; no questions, you are into it.

77　　You make nice gestures throughout the year just because, like love notes on sticky paper left on my bathroom mirror, Hershey's Kisses taped to the fridge door, or balloons tied to my car antenna.

78   You will get up extra early on a freezing weekday morning to shovel the driveway and clear both of our cars of ice and snow, then you start my car for me to warm it up so I don't have to begin my day in a freezing cold car.

79   If I ask you to help me with something, you will stop what you are doing to help.

80   You know the kind of movies and programs I am interested in. You will spend time researching what has come out to see if there is anything I might like. You find out when the programs are available and make sure I get the chance to watch them.

81   You don't engage in stupid activities that work against our relationship when you are out with your friends.

82   It is said everybody has who they *"are"* and who they want to be inside themselves; I feel as though who I *"am"* is *"who"* I want to be when I'm around you. I find this very emotionally productive.

83 You squeeze my butt in the grocery store.

84 You are patient with me.

85 I am lazy. You accept this about me and tell me it creates less stress that you do not have to worry the condition of things all the time.

86 If I am cold, you bring me a blanket or a housecoat; if the occasion requires it, you will give me the coat right off your back.

87 When I choose to go on a diet, you are helpful and supportive, you don't eat snacks around me, you make me tea, even prepare a salad for me while I cook dinner for everyone else.

88   You helped me raise the children I had prior to our relationship and have always treated them as if they were your own.

89   You listen when I need to vent about something.

90   You thank me for the things I do, simple things that are just part of life like, "Thank you for making dinner."

91 You read those relationship - enhancement articles in magazines and listen to relationship-improving tidbits on radio talk shows, if you think something relates to us, you apply it.

92 Just hugging me turns you on.

93 You are rarely ever late for "date night."

94   You leave love notes in my mailbox at work.

95   You bought me a dishwasher because doing the dishes ruined my fingernails, and I wanted to grow them out.

96   You rub my feet when they hurt after work.

Ishtar Silver

97 You hang and fold the laundry that I have washed.

98 I work a lot; you make sure all my favorite programs are recorded so I can watch them at my convenience.

99 If I ask you to turn over while you are sleeping because you are snoring, you will roll over, adjust your pillow, then say, "Sorry baby," from a dead sleep.

100   Sometimes you kiss me good night four or five times.

101   You keep your promises; you don't make a promise if you think there is a remote chance you may not be capable of keeping it.

102   If you get home early from work and I'm still working, you will do chores instead of just watching TV or goofing off on the computer.

Paris Angel

103 You tolerate and interact with my friends being kind and nonjudgmental.

104 You remember every important date in our lives like weddings, birthdays, anniversaries, and the dates of all upcoming special occasions.

105 You ask my opinion about important decisions you have to make that may affect our life.

106 I am a jealous person, and it is truly fine by you; in fact, you consider it a compliment that I get jealous over you at all.

107 Although you are not thrifty with money, you take no offense to the fact that I am, instead, you use that as a positive by having me handle our finances to create more positive.

108   You get a gleam in your eye when you see me headed for the shower. I know what you're thinking . . . *"naked time."*

109   You keep files on your computer of all my favorite music and add to it as I develop more favorites.

110   I have trouble with my back and shoulders; anytime I ask you to rub me for a bit, you do so without hesitation and graciously.

111   You grew your fingernails out so you could give me a good back scratch.

112   You will hang my delicates for me and are in no way offended that they are hanging all over the laundry room.

113   You quit smoking to help me quit smoking.

114   You will bring things to my workplace that I have forgotten at home, like my laptop with the morning's presentation on it.

115   You attend boring, political, group events that my place of employment makes mandatory. You make me look good, impress my superiors, and you always make the most of the occasion, enjoying yourself and people really enjoy you.

116   You still talk about dreams for our future.

117   You make my dinner and serve it to me at my computer while I'm gaming on the weekends.

118   You prepare my meals; I don't even have to think about what is being served. You're a great cook, and I always love what I get.

119   Even though we may have the same days off, you get up and tend the kids, the pets, and the coffee while I sleep in.

120   You laugh at my jokes! I should say my stupid jokes.

121 You smile every time you see me, even if you just saw me ten minutes ago.

122 I have made you late for work more than once . . . in the *good* way.

123 You keep a picture of me on your person while you are traveling.

124 You will leave for work early to have time to drop me off at work so we can get coffee and ride together.

125 You are my buddy, my very best friend!

126 If I ask, "What would you like for dinner?" You will answer, "What's the least amount work for you?" I know you are saying this because you want your evening snuggle time, rather than me spending that time cooking and cleaning.

127   At random you will say, "Let's go for a drive, nothing special, just the two of us in the car going."

128   You bring me tea in bed in the morning on our days off.

129   You offer me the red Skittles.

130   You never pass up a chance to touch me even to the point of brushing by me in the hall or kitchen; if you succeed in physical contact, you make a little noise.

131 You check my tires and car fluids regularly.

Wolf Woman

132 Life has changed little and I have become chubby, in spite of my extra weight I can tell that you still think I'm sexy, you don't tell me how to eat or put me down if I want *dessert*.

133 You tuck me in.

134   My mother likes you.

135 You remember to put the trash curbside on trash day.

136 You know I am a sensitive person, and I like to help people. Even though I have been burned by many people who I have helped, you neither chastise nor discourage me from helping yet another person. Instead, you try to help me to make better decisions about how I can help people without taking such great risks emotionally or financially.

137 You give me a massage at the end of my workday even though you are a massage therapist and have been giving people massages all day long.

Marie

138 If I cook, you clean the kitchen and do the dishes without being asked.

139   You take care of all my computer problems because you are a whiz with computers; there is no procrastination when the computer has a problem, you get right on it.

140   You introduce me to all your friends, coworkers, and family.

141   You share your interests with me because you want me to be a part of the things you enjoy, I can see this when you make an effort to gain my interest so that perhaps I will participate.

142   We are able to laugh at our mistakes in front of each other.

143   We don't argue a lot yet we have our differences, we just respect that we see things in two different lights.

144   When we were first dating you bought me a bottle of wine with dinner and I liked it. To this day on our anniversary you will locate and purchase that same wine for me.

145   Even after a decade of being together we are able to have fun with each other, jest, play, and make jokes with no hard feelings.

146   You will read to me to put me to sleep.

147   You encourage me to learn new things regardless of my age you tell me education is never a waste of time or money.

148 Although you rarely hurt my feelings if you do you apologize with sincerity.

149 You always offer me a bite of your candy bar.

150 You hug me a lot.

151 If you get yourself something while you are running errands like water, energy drink or coffee you always bring one back for me.

152 We work a couple of city blocks apart, you meet me at a local diner every day on our lunch break to talk and have lunch together.

153 You tell me it makes you happy to see me happy.

154 I am in the U.S. Navy. When I have a duty day [24-hour workday] and something amazing has been prepared for dinner, you always save some for me.

155 When you've had a bad day at work, you don't ever take it out on me, instead, you confide in me, rant a bit about the situation to get it off your chest, and then we have a drink or tea together and let it go.

156 You know when to hug me even when I don't know I need a hug.

Wolf Woman

157 I hate to iron, you hate folding laundry and putting it away; you iron, I fold and put away. We often find ourselves in this kind of balance.

158 You respect my car.

159 You make a big spread of goodies for my friends on football or gaming nights.

160 You keep your fingernails and toenails groomed because I like the way it looks.

161   There have been some tough spots in life it seemed we had drifted apart; we went to counseling and found a way to pick up the pieces. We're still together, and we work on our relationship daily. We still laugh, love, and enjoy each other very much.

162   It's just a feeling I get . . . unexplainable!

163   You help me level my characters in video games.

164 Sometimes I look up from what I'm doing to find you just standing there. I ask, "What's going on?" You reply, "Nothing, how about you?" It's an awkward moment like going back in time to when you first liked me. I'm sure you're just standing there looking for an excuse to interact with me.

165 We never sleep on a disagreement or a fight, unless without hostility and upon mutual agreement we see it would benefit us to press pause and resume working it out later.

166   Every year on my birthday you take the day off work to be home, prepare me a nice dinner, and make me a birthday cake.

167   You love *my name*. It is the password for your computer.

168   My lunch is homemade and packed fresh daily; everything from barbecued ribs and coleslaw to grilled chicken Caesar salad. As you are an accomplished chef, I partake in an amazing lunch every day.

169   You brag about me to your friends, family, and coworkers.

170   You cut my hair . . . for *FREE!*

171   I am able to talk to you about anything and not feel like I am being judged.

172   You don't wear your shoes in our house.

173   If something makes me feel better or makes me happier, you feel the need to incorporate it into our lives.

174 You accept my career even though it is a difficult profession to have a relationship in, you give me no grief, and we work things out through compromise.

175 You take every opportunity in life to be my HERO of the day. Big things like driving two hours to sleep by my side even though I'm leaving for home in the morning, and small things like going back to the grocery store where I left my favorite sunglasses to find them. You come through often!

176   You always dress nicely and appropriately for the given occasion when we go out. The only place you are completely casual in shorts, joggers, tank tops, etc., is the place where such clothing applies like the beach, gym, lounging at home, or maybe after surgery.

177   You compliment me often, "Your skin is so soft," "I like your hair like that," "Those jeans look great on you," "You look amazing tonight," and many more.

178   You show your jealousy in an attractive fashion and handle it with grace. I think the fact you still get jealous after all these years speaks for itself.

179   You will press pause on a disagreement we are having and set it aside to be part of a special occasion, such as New Year's, a birthday party, Christmas, or whatever important occasion it is. You will be there and love me in the *NOW*.

Paris Angel

180   Being in the entertainment industry, I am always working during the holidays; you will travel to where I work on New Year's Eve to hang out till the clock strikes midnight just to get your *"NEW YEAR'S KISS."*

181   It is hard for me to fall asleep, and it comforts me to fall asleep beside you. You coordinate your evening schedule to be getting into bed at the same time I do so that we can begin our night's rest together.

182 I love gory movies, lots of blood, guts, mayhem, blowing up things, and car chases . . . I am, however, a woman. You find this attractive and think I'm intriguing when I really get into the action portions of the movie.

183 You appreciate my sense of fashion.

184   You sink your lime in your Corona, turn it once, and then offer me the first cold swill off the top.

185 You run the errands while I'm at work; this way, on our day off, we are sure to have time together.

Wolf Woman

186   Over ten years of being together and you still hold my hand in the movies and while we are walking across parking lots.

187   You still put gum or a mint in your mouth before you kiss me.

188   You know I like a clean tight-made bed, and you will go through the trouble of making it the way I like it even though we are just going to mess it up.

189   You have a picture of me half-dressed on your desk. When people are going to be around this area, you face it down out of respect for me.

190   Even though you're not a very good cook, to give me the night off, you will cook what you can or just order out to get me off my feet for the evening.

191 You get your picture taken with me, and for me, even though you don't like getting your picture taken you know it is important to me.

192 Whenever you have a chance to include me in your business travels, you do. If you have the ability, you will fly me to where you are and we enjoy a sort of mini vacation, even if it's just a couple of days.

193   You never flirt with my friends or coworkers.

194   You have me park in the garage as we only have room for one car; you said you don't like seeing me walk in the rain or spend part of my morning cleaning snow off the car in the cold.

195   You don't pick in the food while I'm cooking; I was brought up that this action is rude, and you respect my feelings about this.

Tender Blue

196   You will make tea for me without me asking because you hear my throat getting a little scratchy.

197   You tell me often . . . I complete you.

198   People think we are newlyweds after all these years of being married.

199   You still whisper sweet nothings in my ear.

200   I really do walk funny the next day.

201   You can make me blush even after all this time.

202   You ask to take me on walks to the park, by the seashore, or just through the neighborhood while we talk about life.

203   You always know the exact right thing to say or do, to make me feel better, no matter what odd set of circumstances I may be fluxing through at that time.

204   You ask me silly little personal questions to get to know more about me.

205   I do most of the cooking, and you love my cooking; you respect the refrigerator and cupboards by never getting into anything that may be part of a recipe.

206   You notice so many things about me not just physical, but emotional as well, sometimes to the point of knowing something about me even before I know it about myself.

207 You don't smoke in our house, our car, or around our children.

208 You like to do things to make me laugh.

209 I am afraid of the dark; you leave night-lights on throughout the house for me and never make fun of my fear.

210   You put movies on at night for me to fall asleep to because I sleep better when there's a movie playing, meanwhile, you wear earplugs to bed.

211   I have a lot of stuff going on with me emotionally, physically, and psychologically. I am never made to feel lesser because of it, instead, you help me in every way you can.

212   I hear from your friends, coworkers, and family members that you talk about me a lot, probably too much, and it's all good things.

213   You treat me as an equal in spite of having much less of an education than you do.

214   You like to sit beside me on the couch better than in a recliner by yourself.

215   You travel a lot for your job. You once flew me to where you were even though you only had twelve hours you could spend with me.

216   My job is cooking; when I come home, dinner is always ready and the mess is clean so I don't have to spend any extra time in the kitchen.

217   You go out of your way to do things that make me proud of you.

218 If you miss my call, you save my message on your voice mail so you can listen to it again later to hear my voice.

219   When I can't reach something up high but I am trying, if you see me doing this, you will say, "Let me get that." You reach over my head and press yourself against me as you reach for whatever it is; there is some kind of gratification for you even in small physical contact with me.

220 You always listen to me when I get inspired and go on ranting about it; you remain very positive about my ideas, offer outside perspective, and ask questions that further stimulate my inspiration.

221 You tolerate my stupid cat (yes, I have a stupid cat, don't all writers?) you are not mean to it, nor do you make it feel unwelcome in our home.

222   Our schedules are very different, you get up a lot earlier than I do; you always make an effort to keep very quiet while you get ready for work so as not to disturb my sleep.

223   Whenever we get in a heated argument, you never say things that hurt real bad or you might regret later.

224   You are not bothered by my delicates drip-drying in the shower.

225   You have pictures of me hanging on your bedroom wall . . . there is nothing else hanging on the walls.

226   Sometimes when I least expect it, you will clean out my car and wash it.

227 You would rather sit beside me in the booth-style seating at a restaurant with your arm around me versus sitting across from me; however you told me sitting across from me has its advantages too because you get to look at me.

228 I can completely be myself around you regardless of which self it is . . . happy, sad, angry, emotional, serious, flirty, tired, energetic, artistic . . . really, the list is endless but because you really dig "*ME*", it's all good!

229   You don't make lame excuses for shit . . . you just say it like it is.

230   You are a very interactive part of our family; you are supportive, positive, loving, understanding, and patient with our children.

231   You take time out of your day if you are available to chauffeur me on errands and appointments when I am not feeling up to driving.

232   You help me to be a better *ME*.

233   You're always trying to find a good movie to entertain me, which is difficult because I am extremely critical and have high expectations of my entertainment, but you keep trying and occasionally succeed.

234   You play with me; roughhouse, tickle, and jest.

235   My mother said you are the best thing that ever happened to me.

236 There is no price for my pleasure; you will go to extremes physically or financially without caring about the cost if it will make me happy.

237   You work out with me at the gym.

238   You watch me while I am sleeping.

239   When you finally met my family, my entire family loved you and you loved my entire family.

240   We both love books; you take me to the library or the bookstore and share book time with me.

241   I am very hard on myself, and you help me to understand myself better because you truly like me; this in turn helps me focus on my positives, which makes me a more productive person.

242 I have a favorite shirt that is old and continually falling apart, instead of throwing it away, you keep repairing it for me.

243 You always leave the last one for me whatever it is.

244 No matter how disappointed I am in myself, you are rarely ever disappointed in me.

245 You never make fun of me because I am fascinated by very simplistic things; instead, you love me more because of it.

246 You support me and my decisions in parenting; you help me become a better parent through your support and understanding.

247 You had my portrait tattooed on your body.

248 You maintain a good influence and are a strong example for our children.

249 My dog loved you from the first moment he met you. My dog was never known for being nice to people he's just met!

250 You verbally praise me for my accomplishments.

251 My father likes you.

252 You catch the same commute home with me so we can share our day and discuss events.

253 You insist on paying for my manicure or pedicure.

254 You text-flirt with me at home, while we are both in the same house.

255   You call the local radio station during after-work traffic to dedicate songs to me while I'm driving home.

256   Whenever I get a cold or am not feeling well, you make homemade chicken soup for me.

257   You make the bed and keep our room tidy.

258   You leave love messages on my voice mail.

259   When you see my IM is up on your computer at any point in the day or night, you will send messages even when we are in the same building.

260   You inspire me to be creative, and you are inspired by me to create.

261   Your presence warms me, your touch calms me, your hug makes me feel secure, your kiss makes me feel whole, I can't imagine I would feel this way about you if you didn't love me enough to make the feeling real.

262 You can't stay mad at me for any length of time.

263 You listen to my inner fears and don't judge me.

Wolf Woman

264 You support my dreams and aspirations; there is no idea I may have about doing something that inspires me that you are not completely behind me in that decision.

265 You tell me I'm beautiful and make me feel so every single day.

Marie

266 You like to comb my hair for me after I get out of the shower.

267 You stop action in a day to kiss me often.

268 When we were first dating, you cleaned your car before taking me out; over a decade later, you still clean the car before taking me anyplace.

269 You take the dogs out in the middle of the night to potty them so I am not outside alone in the dark, cold night.

270 You have a savings account for the sole purpose of gifts for me.

271 You always offer me a bite of your dinner when we go out to eat.

272   When I worked full time and you worked part time, you took care of all the household responsibilities, which gave us more time together.

273   You are a musician and you write songs about me.

274   You bury your face in my hair and take deep long breaths then sigh.

275   You do not chastise my outgoing flirtatious personality, that is who you fell in love with, that is who I am, and that *IS* who you love.

276   When we are separated by business, you will set up your laptop so we can turn on the webcams and see each other while we sleep.

277   You remarried me after our divorce 20 years prior.

278   When you borrow my car, you always put gas in it.

279   You surprise me with gifts on no special occasion. When I ask, "What's the occasion?" You answer, "You are my dear!"

280   You look at me with admiration.

Wolf Woman

281   You make me grilled cheese sandwiches when I'm in a funk; grilled cheese sandwiches remind me of good times during my childhood and wash the funk away.

282   When I come home very late at night after work, I find fresh pajamas and a towel for me on the shower stand in the bathroom.

283   I am not sure I completely understood what a healthy working relationship between two people was until I involved myself with you; I believe it is because you truly love me that makes the difference.

284   You don't lie to me.

285   You always get frisky if you think I'm naked in the bed and will fight me for the blankets to try and find out.

286 We are able to successfully run a business together and work around one another day in and day out and still separate business from our personal life.

287 Anytime you travel away from home, the first thing you do when you get there is call me.

288 You take me on silly dates like dinner in the car while we watch traffic drive by.

289   You still press or dry the flowers I give you.

290   I snore extremely badly, and you still continue to try to find ways to work around it so we can sleep together.

291   You take me out dancing regularly!

292 I finally got my dream job, unfortunately, it moved me to another state; you uprooted your life and moved there to be near me, and you have never made me feel you were unhappy about this decision.

293 No matter where we are, whether it is in an elevator or a major event, you are always there *with* me.

294 Our love life has not become stagnant; it is still very much alive and amazing.

295   Some of the small responsibilities in life you enjoy doing with me, like running odd errands, grocery shopping, cooking, dump runs, and walking the dogs.

296   You take me to do things that I enjoy doing even though you don't really enjoy them, however, you expressed to me that what you do enjoy is seeing me enjoy myself.

297   There will never be enough sunsets over a glass of wine spent together.

Iad Hamdan

298   We go swimming naked together.

299   Even though we live a pretty good distance apart each living in the area we work, after work, you will drive all the way to my place at least three of five work days to spend the night with me.

300 In spite of being divorced, you are still my friend; you keep your word to me and to our children.

301 You love to surprise me.

302 You proposed to me on one knee because you knew I thought this was romantic.

303 You make me things like blankets, hats, pj's, pillows, and house slippers.

304   You buy me books on special occasions rather than cards because they last longer and have more to say.

305   You don't believe there is such a thing as *too* much affection when it comes to me.

306   You cannot get rid of the car we first dated in even though the motor is shot; it still sits in our backyard overgrown with blackberry bushes and covered in moss.

307   People much older than us, as much as two times our age recognize and make comment that we are truly in love.

308   You drive in a way that makes me comfortable as a passenger.

309   I am always adopting, caring for, and feeding stray animals and you never complain; you just smile and bring home another bag of chow.

310 You express to me verbally and regularly things you are grateful for about me.

311   I am a stay at home mom. You respect that, you treat it as a job equal in every way if not more difficult and important than your job, you consider it the foundation of our family, you even help out when you get home and on the weekends.

312   You keep our yard beautiful.

313   You financed my college education.

314   You never make me feel stupid when I cry.

Paris Angel

315   You leave little hearts stickers stuck to things around the house for me.

316   You have a calendar that you count down the days when I'm away on business.

317   I hear you say my name passionately in your sleep.

318   You show off my picture to your friends and coworkers.

319   Our marriage didn't work out, however after the divorce, you started dating me again. We're still dating exclusively, and we have been happily running our relationship like this for many years.

320   You think my quirks are adorable rather than annoying.

321   I am a *BIG* girl, and you appreciate me just the way I am; you think I'm sexy and don't make me feel like I have to be anything different.

322   If we are watching TV together, you don't change the channel before asking if I am interested in what is currently on TV.

323 You keep the fireplace wood chopped and stocked so I don't have to venture into the cold to do so.

324 You had a plane fly a banner for our anniversary.

325 You never leave me without cream for my morning coffee; if we are short, you'll drink yours black.

326   Any dangerous job to be done in our lives you would prefer that you were the one to do it rather than me.

327   You took skydiving lessons with me even though you are afraid of heights.

328   You like to run your fingers through my hair and pet me.

329 You recognize my talents; you encourage and compliment them often.

330 When I'm having a bad time and am short-tempered with everything around me, rather than being upset or short-tempered back, you give me the space I need to work things out.

331   Our lunch breaks are at the same time. I work out at the gym every lunch break. You stop by the gym during your break to check out my butt while I'm on the stair-climber.

332   You will take your lunch or hold a meeting with a client at the restaurant where I work just to be able to see me in the middle of the day.

333   You never miss the opportunity to be physical with me.

Wolf Woman

334   You write love poems to me.

335   You can admit when you're wrong.

336   When we have friend or family gatherings, you always help me with all the work.

337 Not a day goes by that you haven't told me "I love you" at least once.

338 You tell me I am the foundation of your life's purpose.

339 You still place notes on my pillow when you leave; recently, you left one that said, "When I close my eyes, I see your eyes etched on the back of my eyelids."

340 When we've been mad at each other or had an argument, time will go by and you just forget about it or let it go; you don't harbor bad feelings. It's like a magic *mad* eraser that just wipes it away. You don't like to be upset with me, and I don't like to be upset with you, so we work it out fast and efficient.

Paris Angel

341   You pull the car over when I see a wounded animal, and you will help me try to save it even if it can't be saved.

342   You bring home treasures for me from work.

343   Even when you're broke, you find a way to wine and dine me.

344   You got me a puppy so I wouldn't be lonely when you are away.

345 You proposed to *me*.

346 You help me eat healthier without taking everything I like off the menu.

347 You lost the first ring I ever gave you and have spent over a decade looking for its replacement.

348 We still do "*it*" all over our house and places away; here, there, and everywhere.

349   Just before my shift ends at work, you will run an Epsom salt bath for me to soak my legs when I get home because you know they hurt at the end of every shift.

350   You work two jobs so that I am able to be a full-time mom and home school our children; you thank me daily for doing this.

351   There are so many little gestures over the span of a week, even a day that are genuine indications you love me.

352   You light candles around your apartment before I come over.

353   You still open doors, pull out chairs, and take my coat for me.

354   You helped me plan our wedding.

355   I take pictures of many things; I consider it an art form. You never act as though it is a waste of time, nor do you hurry me when I stop to do so. When asked at any given moment, "Will you pull over the car so I can capture something?" you pull over and simply smile as I do.

356   When we are separated by a business trip, you tell me the days seem so much longer.

357   Nights when neither of us has to work, you will make a mat on the floor of the front room, order take out, and put in a movie. You say it's your way of switching things up and getting back to basics.

358   When I put my arms around you from behind, you clasp your hands over my hands like you want me to stay there.

359   You take dance lessons with me.

360   On the nights I work, you always offer to drive me to work if you are not working just to spend those ten minutes on the drive with me, then you'll return to pick me up when I am done for the very same reason.

361   Right about the time I have pushed myself to the brink and I simply feel as though I can't take anymore, you will stop me and say, "Come here, I got you, babe. Take a load off for a minute."

362 When I leave for work in the morning, you always roll over and snuggle my pillow in your sleep.

363 You spoil me.

364 You date me regularly even though we have been married for years.

365 You have a saying,

"Where there is *YOU*, there is magic!"

Iad Hamdan

There are 365 days in each year; there must be millions of simple gestures that express love, care, respect, and approval of your significant other that take very little time but have an immeasurable impact on your relationship with this other person.

Think in different colors and don't allow your heart to be dictated to by society or commercialism. In a world so filled with modern technology, complex working environments, and the dog-eat-dog rat race, which you are required to keep yourself updated with so you can preserve your job, it makes no sense to make love more complicated than it actually is.

Paris Angel

Sometimes the complexity of the most perfect thing is its simplicity.

Now go love simply & simply love.

Paris Angel

Join me at my free web forum for more enriching and alternative ways to share, love, express and enhance relationships and life!

http://www.answersfromparis.com

~~Loving Simply & Simply Loving ~~

Paris Angel

www.ingramcontent.com/pod-product-compliance
Lightning Source LLC
Chambersburg PA
CBHW051651040426
42446CB00009B/1079